W9-CDM-592

Holland Lops

and Other Rabbits

Editor in Chief: Paul A. Kobasa
Supplementary Publications: Christine Sullivan, Scott Thomas
Research: Mike Barr, Cheryl Graham
Graphics and Design: Kathy Creech, Sandra Dyrlund, Tom Evans
Permissions: Loranne K. Shields
Indexing: David Pofelski
Prepress and Manufacturing: Carma Fazio, Anne Fritzinger, Steven Hueppchen
Writer: Sheri Reda

For information about other World Book publications, visit our website at
http://www.worldbook.com or call 1-800-WORLDBK (967-5325).

For information about sales to schools and libraries, call 1-800-975-3250 (United States);
1-800-837-5365 (Canada).

World Book, Inc.
233 N. Michigan Avenue
Chicago, IL 60601
U.S.A.

Library of Congress Cataloging-in-Publication Data

Holland lops and other rabbits.
      p. cm. -- (World Book's animals of the world)
   Summary: "An introduction to Holland lops and other rabbits,
presented in a highly illustrated, question and answer format.
Features include fun facts, glossary, resource list, index, and
scientific classification list"--Provided by publisher.
   Includes bibliographical references and index.
   ISBN-13: 978-0-7166-1330-5
   ISBN-10: 0-7166-1330-1
   1. Leporidae--Juvenile literature. 2. Rabbits--Juvenile literature.
I. World Book, Inc. II. Series.
QL737.L32H65 2007
599.32--dc22
                              2006013232

World Book's Animals of the World
Set 5 ISBN: 978-0-7166-1325-1

Holland Lops and Other Rabbits
Also available as ISBN: 978-0-7166-1579-8 (pbk.)

Printed by Book Partners, a division of the HF Group
North Manchester, Indiana

Picture Acknowledgments: Cover: © Norvia Behling; © David Perry, EcoStock; © Steve Shott, Dorling Kindersley;
© age fotostock/SuperStock.

© Norvia Behling 13, 15, 25, 27 29, 31, 35, 37, 45, 47, 55, 61; © John Daniels, Ardea London 5, 21, 23, 39, 59;
© Renee Morris, Alamy Images 41; © Omlet 19; © David Perry, EcoStock 7; © Joel Sartore 43; © Steve Shott, Dorling
Kindersley 3, 4, 17, 49, 51, 57; © age fotostock/SuperStock 5, 11; © Paul M. Thompson, Alamy Images 53; © Barrie Watts,
Dorling Kindersley 33.

Illustrations: WORLD BOOK illustration by John Fleck 9.

World Book's Animals of the World

Holland Lops
and Other Rabbits

WORLD
BOOK

a Scott Fetzer company
Chicago
www.worldbook.com

Contents

What Is a Rabbit? 6

What Are Those Long Ears For? 8

How Did Breeds of Rabbits Develop? 10

What Kind of Personality Might a Holland Lop Have? 12

What Should You Look For When Choosing a Holland Lop? 14

What Does a Holland Lop Eat? 16

What Plants Are Poisonous to Rabbits,
Including Holland Lops? 18

Where Should a Pet Holland Lop Be Kept? 20

What Is a Good Rabbit Habitat? 22

How Do You Keep the Habitat Healthful? 24

Will a Holland Lop Use a Litter Box? 26

How Do You Groom a Holland Lop? 28

What Kinds of Exercise or Play Are Needed? 30

How Do You Help a Holland Lop Care for Its Young? 32

Who Is the "King" of the Rabbits? 34

Who Is the New Kid on the Block? 36

Which Rabbit Is an Eye-Catcher? 38

Which Is the Tiniest Rabbit? 40

Which Is the Biggest Rabbit of All? 42

How Do Rabbits Communicate? 44

How Should You Pick Up a Rabbit? 46

Do Rabbits Bite? 48

What If Your Rabbit Refuses to Eat? 50

Where Can You Get a Pet Rabbit? 52

What Is a Rabbit Show Like? 54

What Are Some Common Signs of Illness in Rabbits? 56

What Routine Veterinary Care Is Needed? 58

What Are Your Responsibilities as an Owner? 60

Rabbit Fun Facts 62

Glossary 63

Index and Resource List 64

What Is a Rabbit?

Rabbits are mammals—animals that feed their young with milk made by the mother. Rabbits belong to a group of animals called lagomorphs *(LAG uh mawrfz),* which also includes hares. Hares may look a lot like rabbits, but rabbits and hares differ in several ways. For example, rabbits are born unable to see and without fur, while hares are born covered with fur and with their eyes open.

Rabbits may range in size from less than 2 pounds (0.9 kilogram) to more than 16 pounds (7.3 kilograms). Female rabbits, called does *(dohz),* tend to grow larger than male rabbits, called bucks. Rabbits are herbivores *(HUR buh vawz),* or plant-eaters.

Domestic rabbits can live for 10 to 15 years. Wild rabbits do not usually live longer than 6 years. Rabbits can have their first litter of young when they are less than 6 months old.

There are more than 50 breeds of domestic rabbits worldwide. But all domestic rabbits, including Holland Lops, came from the European wild rabbit.

A Holland Lop

7

What Are Those Long Ears For?

The body of a rabbit is much like that of other four-legged animals. Rabbits do have some special features, however.

They often have long, sensitive ears. Many kinds of rabbits use their ears together or one at a time to catch sounds from any direction. The ears also keep the rabbit cool in hot weather by giving off heat.

The long, powerful hind legs are used by a rabbit for hopping. Rabbits also use their powerful back legs for defense, punching with their hind feet.

Rabbits have two pairs of upper incisors (front teeth). One pair is directly behind the other. They use the incisors to gnaw and clip off plants. Then, they chew their food with sideways movements of the lower jaw, which grinds the food and helps wear down the teeth. Their teeth grow all their lives.

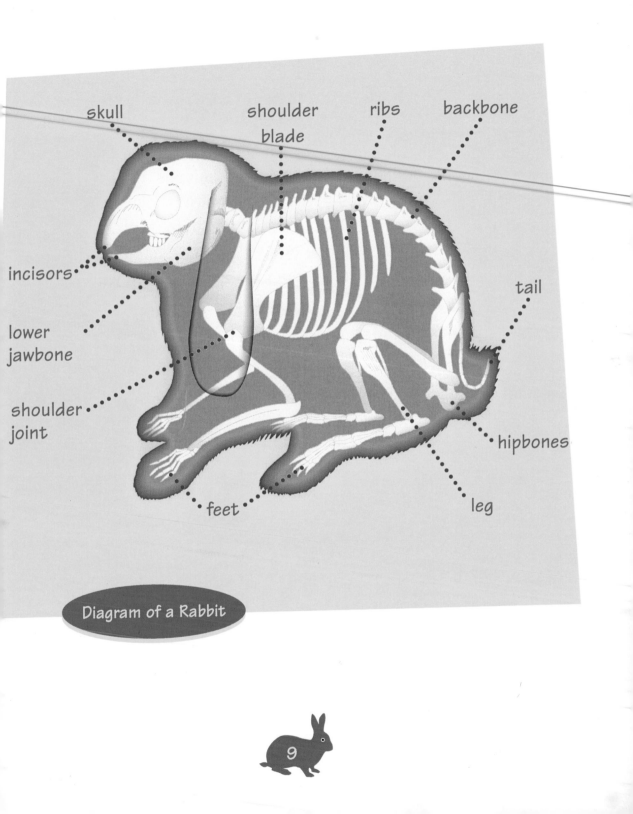

skull

shoulder
blade

ribs

backbone

incisors

lower
jawbone

shoulder
joint

tail

hipbones

feet

leg

Diagram of a Rabbit

How Did Breeds of Rabbits Develop?

People sometimes breed (mate) animals, hoping to develop certain traits (features or characteristics) in the offspring of those animals. When animals are bred to have special traits, the offspring that result are often somewhat different than the animals from which they were bred.

People first bred rabbits for their meat and pelts (skins). Eventually rabbits were also bred for show, and breeders then began to focus on such traits as the quality and color of the animal's fur. Some breeders bred their rabbits to have such traits as long or short hair. Eventually, rabbit breeds—that is, groups of animals that had the same type of ancestors— were developed.

Holland Lops were bred from several different rabbit breeds—Netherland Dwarfs, French Lops, and English Lops. Holland Lops look a little like each of these breeds of rabbits.

Different types of rabbits

What Kind of Personality Might a Holland Lop Have?

Holland Lops can display many different types of personalities.

Some Holland Lops are so calm and quiet that they rarely move. They will allow you to pet them, but they do not seem very interested in interaction with humans. Other Holland Lops are nervous and restless. They run around a lot, mark their territory, and sometimes even bite.

Many Holland Lops, however, have the perfect personality to be pets. These lops are lively and curious, but cuddly and cute. Although they are playful, they love to be petted. They will pose for a judge in a show, and they will show affection toward other animals.

When you look for a Holland Lop as a pet, be sure it has a personality that you will enjoy.

A Holland Lop grooming

13

What Should You Look For When Choosing a Holland Lop?

If you want to give a Holland Lop a home, take some time to get to know the animal. Notice whether the rabbit comes to greet you, and make sure it is active, with bright eyes and a shiny coat of fur.

If you are interested in a particular rabbit, get permission to pet it. Check its body to feel for lumps or swellings, which may be caused by parasites, such as ticks. Also, look for scabs, infected cuts, and scratches.

Make sure the rabbit's teeth close just as human teeth usually do: top over bottom. And make sure the rabbit has four toes on each foot and a dewclaw (a small inner toe that does not reach the ground) on each front foot.

Finally, ask for a guarantee or a 72-hour return policy so you can have a veterinarian check your rabbit to be sure it is healthy.

Young Holland Lops

What Does a Holland Lop Eat?

A Holland Lop needs a well-balanced diet. Many experts recommend feeding rabbits pellets made from a grass hay, such as timothy, oat, brome, or Bermuda grass, but not from alfalfa. Also, provide as much fresh grass hay as your rabbit wants to eat. The fresh hay provides fiber and helps keep the teeth healthy. Finally, your rabbit should have some fresh green vegetables, such as broccoli, carrot tops, endive, or parsley. Some people feed their rabbit these types of vegetables daily, while others make these vegetables a treat served in addition to a pellet and hay diet.

Some people don't feed their rabbits any pellet food. They feed them a diet of only fresh hay, vegetables, and some fruit. If you decide to do this, you must check with your veterinarian to make sure your rabbit gets all the nutrients it needs.

The proper food is important to a rabbit's diet, but water is just as important. Make certain that your pet always has plenty of fresh water to drink.

16

A lop enjoying dried food

What Plants Are Poisonous to Rabbits, Including Holland Lops?

Many kinds of plants or parts of plants are poisonous to Holland Lops and other rabbits. These plants include aloe vera, apple and pear seeds, ivy, daffodil and tulip bulbs, mustard root, and beans.

So how do you keep your rabbit safe? Make sure that you "rabbit proof" the places where you let your bunny play. Keep household plants and leftover foods out of your rabbit's reach. Outdoors, restrict your rabbit to areas where all the plants are safe to eat.

Most importantly, never give your rabbit any food you have not checked out for safety. Just because it is safe for cats, dogs, or people does not mean it is okay for rabbits.

An outdoor enclosure keeps a rabbit safe

19

Where Should a Pet Holland Lop Be Kept?

Wild rabbits enjoy the outdoors, of course, but a pet usually prefers to live indoors. Pet rabbits can easily become ill when they are exposed to extreme weather.

If you keep your Holland Lop indoors, you will need to "bunny-proof" your home so that your rabbit can be safe when it is out of its cage. Keep wires, cables, and all kinds of cords out of your rabbit's reach, or place these items inside plastic tubing or spiral cable wrap.

Keep your pet safe by placing such electronic devices as remote controls, and any other chewable items, out of reach. To keep your bunny from chewing on woodwork and furniture, buy plastic covers for baseboards and wrap furniture legs in thick plastic. To keep your pet rabbit safe and out of trouble, keep it busy with safe and interesting toys to play with (see page 30).

A lop in an
indoor cage

What Is a Good Rabbit Habitat?

A habitat is a place where an animal lives, which contains everything the animal needs. A pet has a habitat of sorts, provided by its owner. A pet rabbit needs a hutch, or rabbit cage, in an area that provides shelter against wind, rain, cold drafts, and hot sun. Rabbits need to remain out of direct sunlight or temperatures above 80 °F (27 °C) at all times.

The cage should be long enough for the rabbit to stretch out comfortably and tall enough for the rabbit to sit up. Larger would be better. If a rabbit must be kept in a smaller cage, it should be allowed daily playtime outside its cage.

Line the bottom of your rabbit's cage with enough bedding of fresh hay or straw to allow your pet to dig. A litter box is a good idea if your pet has been taught to use it. The litter absorbs some of the ammonia from your pet's urine and helps to keep its cage cleaner. If you provide your pet with a litter box, fill the box with a safe litter made of paper or alfalfa pellets.

Putting down bedding in a rabbit hutch

How Do You Keep the Habitat Healthful?

To keep your rabbit's home comfortable and healthful, keep it ventilated, clean, shady, and not too hot or cold.

For your pet's comfort and health, the bedding at the bottom of its cage should be changed every other day or so, depending on how dirty the litter gets. If your pet is litter-trained, you may be able to keep bedding for up to a week. However, you must then change the litter in the litter box every day or two.

For feeding, you will need a small dog bowl or 4-inch (10-centimeter) crock in the habitat. Many owners attach the feeding bowl to the side of the cage. Some owners also suggest using a hayrack to keep the rabbit's hay clean and ready to eat.

A slightly larger crock can serve as a water bowl. Many owners, however, prefer to use a feeder bottle—a bottle that hangs from the side of the cage and that dispenses water.

A Holland Lop eating
hay from a rack

Will a Holland Lop Use a Litter Box?

Rabbits, including Holland Lops, do not automatically use a litter box, as cats usually will. Still, rabbits do like to set aside a particular spot where they relieve themselves. You can use this behavior on the part of a rabbit to help train your pet to use a litter box.

First, please note, the chemicals in most cat litters are dangerous for rabbits. Further, litters made from such wood products as pine or cedar can be harmful to rabbits. Any litter used in a rabbit litter box should be an organic litter made from such things as paper or alfalfa, which are safe for rabbits.

To train your rabbit, notice where your pet has made a "potty-spot" in its cage. Then, fill a litter box with a safe type of litter and place the box in that spot. Also, put a few of the rabbit's droppings into the litter box so that the box looks and smells familiar to your pet. If you see your rabbit use its box, immediately give the rabbit a treat and praise it. Soon your rabbit may be using its litter box all the time.

A lop
in its litter box

27

How Do You Groom a Holland Lop?

Although rabbits clean themselves by licking their fur, they have a lot of fur. So, do your rabbit a favor and help out with the grooming. At least once a week, go over your Holland Lop's fur with a bristle brush, slicker brush, or damp washcloth. Then, use a flea comb to remove tangles in its fur. This grooming does more than just help your Holland Lop to look nice. It helps loosen and remove old hair and skin and increases blood flow to the skin, which should bring a shine to your pet's coat of fur!

Rabbits very rarely need a bath and should only be bathed when really necessary. Instead of bathing your rabbit, a better idea is to "spot clean" your rabbit—that is, just clean the spot that is dirty with a warm, wet washcloth.

When your pet's nails get long, ask an adult to trim them with well-sharpened nail clippers designed for use on small animals. Be careful not to get the nails too short.

A Holland Lop
being brushed

What Kinds of Exercise or Play Are Needed?

Like all rabbits, Holland Lops need exercise. Fortunately they love to run and play.

Holland Lops often enjoy playing a game of "tag" or "hide-and-seek." (But, make sure your pet does not hide too well.)

Rabbits also like to play with safe rabbit toys. You can roll a ball around the yard and let your rabbit explore or set out blocks of wood that your pet can climb on and chew.

Holland Lops are curious about paper bags, cardboard boxes, and cardboard tubes from paper towels. Rabbits also enjoy playing in sandboxes, and they love to explore different kinds of hideouts.

To help your rabbit play safely, clear a room of dangers or put up a portable fence. Then, invite your Holland Lop out of its cage for playtime!

A Holland Lop with a toy

How Do You Help a Holland Lop Care for Its Young?

Female Holland Lops can have young, called kits, at any time of year. When a Holland Lop is expecting kits, she will be especially hungry and thirsty. Give her plenty of food and water during this time.

About a week before she expects her kits, a doe will make a nest. You can help out by putting a nest box in her cage. Several days later, she will give birth to a litter of three or four kits.

A mother rabbit nurses, or feeds her own milk, to her kits for only a few weeks. The kits should stay in her cage until she stops nursing them, and they should not be handled much.

Once she has stopped nursing, the kits can go to a new home—with another family or in a cage next door to their mother's cage.

Newborn kits in a nest

33

Who Is the "King" of the Rabbits?

One rabbit has fur so beautiful, it was named Rex, the Latin word for "king."

Most breeds of rabbit have beautiful, soft fur, but the Rex rabbit's fur is exceptionally soft. It is extra fine and very short, so this rabbit looks and feels like velvet. In rabbit shows, Rex rabbits are judged on their fur rather than on other physical qualities.

Nevertheless, Rex rabbits have many other good qualities. A Rex is a fairly large rabbit and is less jumpy than smaller rabbits, so a Rex can be easier to handle. Rex rabbits are also very intelligent and playful.

Mini Rex rabbits, which are smaller versions of standard Rex rabbits, are sometimes called Velveteen rabbits. They are named for the cuddly rabbit in the storybook by Margery Williams, *The Velveteen Rabbit.*

A Mini Rex rabbit

 35

Who Is the New Kid on the Block?

One newer breed of rabbit is called the Lionhead. Lionhead rabbits have a special, unforgettable feature. Both male and female Lionheads have a mane of "wool." (Very long fur on rabbits is known as wool.) This mane encircles the rabbit's head and makes the rabbit look like a small lion.

Lionheads have been a recognized breed in the United Kingdom since 2002. In the United States, breeders began showing the Lionhead in 2004. According to the associations that regulate rabbit breeds, Lionhead rabbits should have ears that stand up straight. (There is, however, a lop-eared version of a Lionhead that is not yet recognized by the rabbit associations.)

Lionheads are friendly and easy to train and care for. Since most of their fur is not wool, they do not need as much grooming as other wool breeds, such as Angoras (see page 42).

A Lionhead rabbit

37

Which Rabbit Is an Eye-Catcher?

The Blanc de Hotot *(hoh toh)* has one truly noticeable feature—its eyes.

This breed of rabbit has a round body, a round head, and short ears. Its fur is white. This white fur allows the dark fur that encircles the eye of the Hotot to really stand out. The fur around the eye is called an eyeband.

The Blanc de Hotot (white of Hotot) was developed in the early 1900's in Hotot-en-Auge, in France. A dwarf version of the Hotot breed developed in Germany in the late 1970's. The full-sized Hotot weighs between 8 to 11 pounds (3.6 to 5 kilograms). The dwarf version weighs under 3 pounds (1.4 kilograms).

A Blanc de Hotot

Which Is the Tiniest Rabbit?

There are miniature versions of many rabbit breeds. For example, Holland Lops have smaller relatives known as Mini Lops, and there is a smaller version of a Rex rabbit called a Mini Rex.

Some breeds, however, are small by nature. For example, Netherland Dwarf rabbits remain very small throughout their lives. Adult Netherland Dwarfs usually weigh less than 2 pounds (0.9 kilogram). These tiny, short-haired rabbits often look like furry little balls. Netherland Dwarfs come in many colors, ranging from white to deepest black.

Netherland Dwarfs are extremely cute—but they can be cranky. This breed is sometimes prone to biting. That is why some breeders advise people who are considering a rabbit for a pet to admire the Netherland Dwarfs—but find some other, less aggressive rabbit for a pet.

A Netherland Dwarf
(right) with a guinea pig

Which Is the Biggest Rabbit of All?

Not all rabbits are cute and tiny. Some are cute and rather large.

Angoras (a type of rabbit with long fur), for example, are usually medium- to large-sized, compared with other rabbits. But Giant Angoras, all of which are white, can weigh in at 10 pounds (4.5 kilograms) or more when fully grown. Mature French Lops also weigh about 10 pounds.

The Giant Chinchilla, a breed of rabbit that has a reputation as a sweet-tempered pet, weighs between 12 and 16 pounds (5.4 and 7.3 kilograms) fully grown, as does a rabbit breed known as the Giant Papillon.

Flemish Giants, however, are the breed of rabbit that can grow the largest. Long and heavy, mature Flemish Giants can weigh up to 17 pounds (8 kilograms).

A Flemish Giant

How Do Rabbits Communicate?

Rabbits use their bodies to communicate with each other.

For example, many types of rabbits press their ears back when endangered. Holland Lops cannot do that, but they do crouch into as small a ball as possible.

If rabbits are very frightened, they may thump the ground with a back foot to communicate that danger is near. If a rabbit grunts or growls, it is annoyed. In rare instances, it may even attack.

If a rabbit begins running and jumping straight up in the air and twisting, that is a sign of panic. If it screams, a rabbit is very frightened or in pain. Take steps right away to protect the rabbit and make it feel safe.

When a rabbit lies on its side or its belly with its back legs spread out behind it, a rabbit is feeling safe and secure. A contented rabbit might also purr, make clicking sounds, or softly grind its teeth.

A Holland Lop communicating contentment

How Should You Pick Up a Rabbit?

Rabbits are squirmy creatures, but if your pet feels safe, it will relax contentedly in your arms.

To pick up your rabbit, find a spot next to its habitat where you can sit or kneel comfortably. Place one hand under your rabbit's rump, or hindquarters, to support it. With the other hand, grab the rabbit quickly and gently by the scruff, or back of its neck. Lift up your rabbit with both hands so it feels supported and balanced.

Now place your pet against your body, with all four of its feet resting on your chest or lap. Keep one hand under its rump so that your pet does not dangle dangerously. Take the other hand off the scruff of the neck and cover your rabbit's ears—if the ears wobble, so will the bunny.

If your rabbit is very shy, ask an adult to wrap it in a towel or baby blanket before handing it to you. This will make your pet will feel extra cozy and secure.

46

The proper way to
pick up a rabbit

Do Rabbits Bite?

Rabbits do not usually bite. They will, however, chew on food, toys, wood, and anything else that they think is food. So if you stick your finger into your rabbit's cage, it might nip at your finger. And, if that finger is sweet-smelling and sticky, your rabbit might try to munch it.

Sometimes, rabbits will also nibble on clothes. If you tell your rabbit "no" and give your pet something that is okay to chew on, it should stop nibbling on you.

If your rabbit becomes frightened or annoyed, it will try to run away or hide. If it cannot get away, a scared or angry rabbit will lower its head, charge, and try to scratch with its claws. Most rabbits only bite as a last resort.

A rabbit gnawing on a stick

What If Your Rabbit Refuses to Eat?

Rabbits, especially Holland Lops, can be picky eaters. Before you assume something is wrong with your pet, make sure your rabbit's water bottle works properly. Then check to see that the water in it is cool and clean.

If your rabbit is drinking but not eating, make sure that its food is appetizing. Clean out its feeder to make sure it is free of dust and mold. Also make sure the food pellets are fresh and dry.

If your pet still does not eat, remove all food pellets for a day and offer your rabbit plenty of hay and water. Your rabbit may have a hairball in its stomach. Rabbits get hairballs from licking their fur when grooming and then swallowing that fur. A fur ball can cause a rabbit to refuse food and to have a difficult time eliminating solid wastes. Feeding your rabbit a lot of fresh hay and water can help the rabbit to pass this blockage.

If your rabbit refuses food for 48 hours, call a veterinarian. A serious blockage or other illness may require care right away.

Filling a rabbit's water bottle

Where Can You Get a Pet Rabbit?

Many rabbit owners get their animals from shelters or rescue groups. These organizations save unwanted animals from being killed. The organizations often charge very little money and sometimes include medical treatment and spaying or neutering in the price.

Reliable breeders are another source for breeds of pet rabbits, including Holland Lops. Breeders can offer advice on caring for a rabbit.

Some 4-H programs, Future Farmers of America (FFA) organizations, and Scout troops also sell rabbits. Often, these sellers will know all about their animals and can help you make an informed choice. They also may charge less than a breeder would.

You can also try a pet store—but make sure the store's owners know and care about rabbits. Choose a store with experience in dealing with rabbits.

Rabbits at a shelter
awaiting a home

What Is a Rabbit Show Like?

At rabbit shows, animals are judged on which is the best of a certain breed of rabbits. Each animal is judged according to standards set for its breed. In the United States and Canada, the American Rabbit Breeders Association (ARBA) sponsors many of these shows.

How can you find out if your pet rabbit is a prize winner? You can study ARBA standards, train your rabbit, enter a contest, and find out. The ARBA has a youth division in which people younger than 19 years of age compete. Pet rabbits are also judged at 4-H competitions.

A Lionhead rabbit at a
4-H competition

What Are Some Common Signs of Illness in Rabbits?

Rabbits are usually fairly healthy. But, even healthy rabbits are prone to a few kinds of problems. Rabbits often cut or scratch themselves. They also get hairballs from grooming their fur. And they are likely at some point to get diarrhea, colds, and bacterial infections. Lop-eared rabbits are especially likely to get ear infections.

Minor rabbit illnesses are easy to treat. Antibiotic ointment protects cuts and scratches. Hay and water, as well as fresh papaya or pineapple, can help rabbits to pass hairballs. Whole wheat bread, dry oatmeal, and hay can cure mild diarrhea caused by too many fresh fruits and vegetables in your rabbit's diet. Your vet can give you medicine to treat colds and minor infections your rabbit might catch.

If any illness or condition bothers your rabbit for more than a day, call your vet. Long-lasting illnesses can kill your pet.

Comforting a rabbit

57

What Routine Veterinary Care Is Needed?

Even healthy rabbits can benefit from a visit to the veterinarian now and then. All rabbits should get regular checkups, including dental checkups, to make sure they are well. Your vet can tell you how often these routine checkups should happen. At each checkup, the vet can check for parasites and look for other problems you may not have noticed.

In addition, pet rabbits should be spayed or neutered. Spaying (for females) or neutering (for males) ensures that your rabbit will not produce offspring that you cannot take care of. Spay or neuter also helps keep pet rabbits calm, friendly, and less likely to run away.

Experienced vets are a good source of advice about your pet. They can help you adjust your rabbit's diet or its living space to keep it active, healthy, and happy in its home with you.

A veterinarian
examining a rabbit

59

What Are Your Responsibilities as an Owner?

Holland Lops and other domestic rabbits are not endangered (in danger of dying out). Nevertheless, pet rabbits do need to be cared for in a loving, responsible way. Before you buy a rabbit, think about the daily and weekly care it will require. Do not forget that the cute little bunny you see in the pet store will grow up to be a larger rabbit that needs to run, jump, and play.

Remember that rabbits do not know which items in a home are off-limits. It is up to you to keep them safe from dangers and to keep valuable items out of their reach. And, when outside, your rabbit must be in an enclosure that prevents it from getting lost or being hurt by wild animals.

Also, remember that not all pet animals get along with each other right away. Keep other pets—even other rabbits—away from a new pet rabbit until you are sure they will all get along.

Rabbits in an outdoor enclosure

61

Rabbit Fun Facts

→ Domestic rabbits are born blind and hairless.

→ In the wild, European rabbits will often live together in large colonies, sharing a large system of underground burrows, called warrens.

→ A pika is a small furry relative of rabbits and hares. The pika, however, looks more like a mouse or guinea pig than a rabbit.

→ The Latin name for the Iberian Peninsula—where Spain and Portugal are located—is named for a term in the ancient language of Phoenician that meant "rabbit land."

→ The children of two United States presidents had pet rabbits in the White House—Abraham Lincoln and John Kennedy.

→ In Japan, and in other Eastern cultures, people do not imagine a "man in the moon." Instead, they look for a "rabbit in the moon!"

Glossary

breed To produce animals by carefully selecting and mating them for certain traits. Also, a group of animals having the same type of ancestors.

buck A male rabbit.

dewclaw In rabbits and some other animals, a small inner toe that does not reach the ground.

doe A female rabbit.

domestic A tame animal living with or under the care of humans. Cats, dogs, and rabbits are some examples of domestic animals.

habitat The area where an animal lives, which contains everything the animal needs to survive.

herbivore An animal that feeds on grass or other plants.

hutch A box or pen for small animals.

kit A young rabbit.

lagomorph A member of an order of mammals. The order consists of rabbits, hares, and pikas. Lagomorphs are similar to rodents.

mammal A type of animal that feeds its young with milk made by the mother.

mane The long, heavy hair on the back of or around the neck of certain animals.

neuter To operate on a male animal to make it unable to produce young.

parasite An organism (living creature) that feeds on and lives on or in the body of another organism, often causing harm to the being on which it feeds.

rump The hind part of the body of an animal, where the legs join the back.

scruff The skin at the back of the neck.

spay To operate on a female animal to make it unable to have young.

trait A feature or characteristic particular to an animal or breed of animals.

Index

(**Boldface** indicates a photo or illustration.)

American Rabbit Breeders Association (ARBA), 54

bedding, 22, **23**, 24
breeders, of rabbits, 52
breeds, 10, **11**
bucks, 6

cages. *See* habitats

does, 6, 32

ears, 8
eyebands, 38, **39**

feeding, 16, **17**; avoiding poisons, 18; problems with, 50; things needed for, 24, **25**
4-H competitions, 54, **55**

grooming, 28, **29**

habitats: good, 22, **23**; indoor, 18, 20, **21**; keeping healthful, 24; outdoor, 18, **19**, 60, **61**. *See also* litter boxes
hairballs, 50, 56
hares, 6, 62
herbivores, 6
Holland Lops, 6, **7, 13, 15**; breeding of, 10; care of young by, 32, **33**; choosing, 14; communication by, 44, **45**; enclosures for, *see* habitats;

exercise and play for, 30, **31**; feeding, *see* feeding; grooming, 28, **29**; litter box for, 22, 26, **27**; owners' responsibilities toward, 60; personalities of, 12; plants poisonous to, 18; relatives of, 40; where to get, 52
hutches. *See* habitats

Iberian Peninsula, 62
Illness, in rabbits, 14, 50, 56, **57, 58**
incisors, 8, **9**

kits, 32, **33**

lagomorphs, 6
litter boxes, 22, 24, 26, **27**

manes, 36, **37**

nails, clipping of, 28
neutering, 58

parasites, 14, 58
pet stores, 52
pikas, 62
plants, poisonous, 18

rabbits, 6; Angora, 36, 42; biting by, 12, 48, **49**; Blanc de Hotot, 38, **39**; breeds of, 6, 10, **11**; communication by, 44, **45**;

domestic, 6; ears of, 8; enclosures for, *see* habitats; English Lop, 10; fear in, 12, 44, 48; feeding, *see* feeding; Flemish Giant, 42, **43**; French Lop, 10, 42; fun facts on, 62; Giant Angora, 42; Giant Chinchilla, 42; Giant Papillon, 42; how to pick up, 46, **47**; illness in, 14, 50, 56, **57**, 58; Lionhead, 36, **37, 55**; Mini Lop, 40; Mini Rex, 34, **35**, 40; Netherland Dwarf, 10, 40, **41**; owners' responsibilities toward, 60; parts of, 8, **9**; Rex, 34, 40; sizes of, 6, 40, **41**, 42, **43**; Velveteen, 34, 40; veterinary care for, 14, 50, 56, 58, **59**; where to get, 52, **53**; wild, 6. *See also* Holland Lops
rabbit shows, 10, 14, 54, **55**
rescue groups, 52

scruff, 46, **47**
shelters, rabbits from, 52, **53**
spaying, 58

teeth, 8, **9**

veterinarians, 14, 50, 56, 58, **59**

warrens, 62
"wool," on rabbits, 36, **37**

For more information about Holland Lops and Other Rabbits, try these resources:

Dwarf Rabbits, by Monika Wegler, Barron's Educational Series, 1998

House Rabbit Handbook: How to Live with an Urban Rabbit, 4th edition, by Marinell Harriman, Drollery Press, 2005

Lop Rabbits as Pets, by Sandy Crook, TFH Publications, 1989

The Rabbit: An Owner's Guide to a Happy Healthy Pet, 2nd edition, by Audrey Pavia, Howell Book House, 1996

http://www.arba.net/
http://www.hlrsc.com/
http://www.rabbit.org/adoption/index.html
http://www.rabbitweb.net/

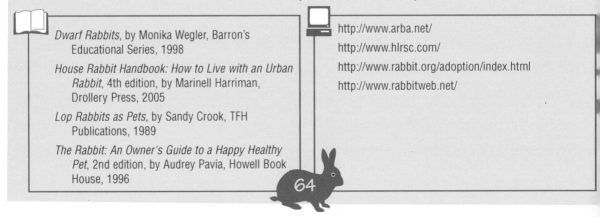